HOW TO MAKE 'EM LAUGH

JOKE

BOOK

Other Smarties titles available

Smarties Book of Wizardry
Smarties Chuckle Factory
Smarties Dinosaur Jokes
Smarties Hilariously Funny Verse
Smarties How to Draw Cartoons
Smarties Joke Book
Smarties Smart Art
Smarties Smart Science
Smarties Travel Teasers

Nestlé SMARTIES HOW TO MAKE 'EM LAUGH JOKE BOOK

JUSTIN SCROGGIE

Illustrated by David Mostyn

Robinson Children's Books

Constable & Robinson Ltd
3 The Lanchesters
162 Fulham Palace Road
London
W6 9ER

First published in the UK by Robinson Children's Books,
an imprint of Constable & Robinson Ltd, 2001

A copy of the British Library Cataloguing in Publication Data
for this title is available from the British Library

ISBN 1-84119-311-9

Printed and bound in the EC

10 9 8 7 6 5 4 3 2 1

Contents

Introduction

What do you get if you cross
a really funny joke book with
a book that shows you how jokes are made with
a book all about making up your own jokes?!

The Smarties HOW TO MAKE 'EM LAUGH Joke Book!

Yes, this is the first ever joke book to tell you everything you need to know to tell jokes, understand jokes and make up your own jokes. In fact, the HOW TO MAKE 'EM LAUGH Joke Book is THREE fabulous books in one volume!

FIRST, it's jam-packed with fantastic jokes of all types. Each TYPE of joke has its own special chapter.

⇨ **TYPES OF JOKE!**
Select

Light Bulb!	Teacher & Pupil
If You Cross!	Stupid!
Waiter, Waiter!	Limerick
Mummy, Mummy!	Doctor, Doctor!
Knock, Knock!	On the Head!

SECOND, each chapter shows you HOW jokes are made using a SECRET FORMULA.

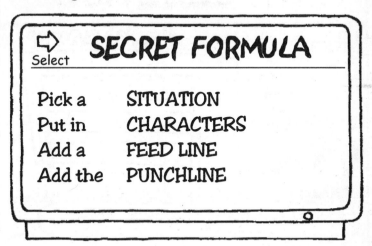

➡ Select

SECRET FORMULA

Pick a	SITUATION
Put in	CHARACTERS
Add a	FEED LINE
Add the	PUNCHLINE

THIRD, YOU get a chance to make up your OWN jokes!

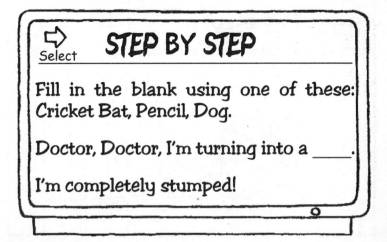

➡ Select

STEP BY STEP

Fill in the blank using one of these: Cricket Bat, Pencil, Dog.

Doctor, Doctor, I'm turning into a ____.

I'm completely stumped!

The Secret Formula

We reveal for the very first time the TOP SECRET FORMULA for making jokes. Don't tell everyone!

SELECT A SITUATION
where the joke happens.

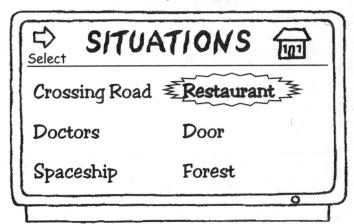

PUT IN CHARACTERS
they're the actors in the joke.

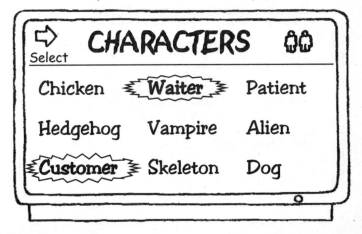

ADD A FEED LINE
this prepares you for the big funny line.

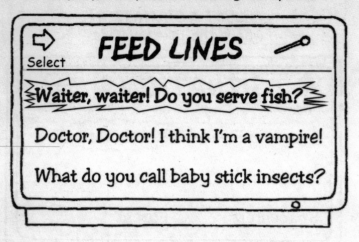

FEED LINES

Select

Waiter, waiter! Do you serve fish?

Doctor, Doctor! I think I'm a vampire!

What do you call baby stick insects?

ADD THE PUNCHLINE
this hits you on the head and makes you laugh!

PUNCHLINES

Select

We serve anyone, sir!

Necks, please!

Twiglets!

Put them all TOGETHER . . .

And you've made a JOKE!

Customer: Waiter, Waiter! Do you serve snails?
Waiter: We serve anyone, sir!

JOKES CAN BE LONG

This guy went into the doctor's, and stood to attention in front of him. "How can I help you?" asked the doctor. "I think I'm turning into a grandfather clock," said the man. The doctor looked at the man for several minutes. "I must say," said the doctor at last, "you're very old, very tall, very striking, and have a round face. I think you're right!" The man looked horrified. "But, doctor, you don't really think I'm turning into a grandfather clock, do you?" The doctor smiled broadly. "No, I was just winding you up!"

OR SHORT

Doctor, Doctor,
those pills you gave me yesterday are shrinking!
I know, Mrs Jones, they're slimming pills.

IN VERSE

There was a young fellow called Fred,
Who went to the doctor's and said:
"I keep taking a shower,
'cos I'm covered in flour."
"Do not fear," said the Doc, "you're well-bred!"

OR IN A CARTOON

Cross the Road!

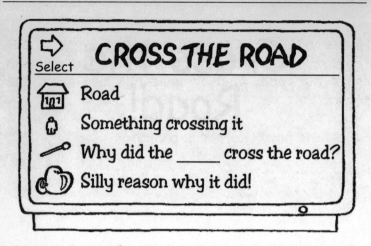

Why did the chicken cross the road?
To get to the other side!

This is one of the OLDEST jokes in the world. It's so old, the dinosaurs may have died out from laughing at it!

So why is it funny? Well, there's just something funny about chickens! They strut about looking very important and very busy. In fact they're very STUPID.

Here's STUPID: Chickens have got wings — but they walk everywhere! So why did the chicken cross the road, when it could FLY and avoid the traffic?

Scientists have another explanation:

Why did the chicken cross the road?
Because chickens need to eat
gravel to digest their food properly.

'Cross-the-road' jokes are about doing an ordinary thing for a *silly* reason:

Why did the chicken cross the road,
and come straight back again?
His braces got caught round a lamp-post!

Why did the Puss cross the road?
He wanted to go in Boots!

Why did the calf cross the road?
To get to the udder side!

My favourite 'cross-the-road' joke isn't a 'road' joke at all. But it's very funny anyway:

My son's a terrible Boy Scout.
How come?
He keeps helping old ladies across the road.
Halfway!

PERFORMANCE
TIP:
Learn 3 or 4 'cross-the-road' jokes — they're funnier in a group. The first joke should have a 'chicken' in it.

PS Which jokes do chickens like best?
Corny ones!

PICK YOUR PUNCHLINE!

Know a good punchline? Try to match each feed line
to one of the punchlines, then turn the page to see
if you were a right comedian!

Why did the chicken go *halfway* across the road?
It was tired!
It had one leg!
It wanted to lay it on the line!

Why did the chicken tell a cross-the-road joke?

It was her favourite joke!
She was a comedi-hen!
It was the monster's day off!

Why did the unwashed chicken cross the road
twice?

It was a dirty double-crosser!
To get to the bathroom!
She changed her mind!

YOU CRACKED IT!

Why did the chicken go *halfway* across the road?
It wanted to lay it on the line!

Why did the chicken tell a cross-the-road joke?
She was a comedi-hen!

Why did the unwashed chicken cross the road
twice?
It was a dirty double-crosser!

PICK YOUR PUNCHLINE!

Why did the chicken jump across the road?

She saw the zebra crossing!
She was a spring chicken!
To get to the blood bank!

Why did the duck cross the road?

Dunno, it must have been quackers!
It forgot to duck!
To get to Boots!

Why did the fish cross the road so fast?

It was the chicken's day off!
To get to the hover side!
It was riding a motor pike!

YOU CRACKED IT!

Why did the chicken jump across the road?
She was a spring chicken!

Why did the duck cross the road?
Dunno, it must have been quackers!

Why did the fish cross the road so fast?
It was riding a motor pike!

NOW MAKE 'EM LAUGH!

Why did the chewing gum cross the road?
It was stuck to the chicken's foot!

Why did the chick cross the road?
To get to its mother's side!

Why did the dead chicken cross the road?
To get to the Other Side!

Why did the alien cross the road?
He saw the green man flashing!

Why did the skeleton cross the road?
To get to the Body Shop!

Why didn't the skeleton cross the road?
He was bone idle!

Why didn't the other skeleton cross the road?
She didn't have the guts!

Why did the vampire cross the road?
To get to the blood bank!

Why didn't the wasp cross the road?
Because it was a B Road!

Why did the rabbit cross the road?
To get to the hare dresser!

Why did the water rat cross the road?
To get to the otter side!

Why did the frog cross the road?
It was following the Green Cross Toad!

Why did the stupid man cross the road?
What ro——?

Why did the oven cross the road?
He saw the microwave!

Why did the cat cross the road?
He was in a fowl mood!

Why did the puzzler cross the road?
She wanted 2 across!

Why did the chicken pox cross the road?
It was rash hour!

Why did the fox chase the hen across the road?
He wanted to see *Chicken Run*!

Why did the chicken cross the A1?
To get to Hen-don!

Why did the polar bear cross the road?
He was Ice-Treat shopping!

Why did the pig cross the road?
He was a road hog!

Why did the chicken cross the fairground?
To get to the other ride!

Why did the chicken cross the yellow brick road?
Because, because, because, because, because!

Why did the French hen cross the road?
To get to the French Henbassy!

Why did the banana skin cross the road?
It was a slip road!

Why did the robot cross the road?
It was an electrode!

Why did the rubber chicken cross the road?
To stretch its legs!

Why did the railway bridge cross the road?
So the trains miss the cars, idiot!

Why did the zoo keeper cross the road?
To get to the yellow lion!

Why did the drunk zoo keeper cross the road?
To get to the double yellow lion!

Why did the football team cross the road?
To play the other side!

Why did the chocolate cross the road?
To get to Quality Street!

Difference
Between!

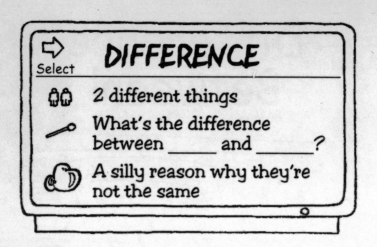

Just putting two DIFFERENT things together can be very funny. Imagine a tiny dog sitting on a huge flea, or a fish playing the piano!
Now ask yourself WHY they're different:

What's the difference
between a dog and a flea?

There are lots of differences between a dog and a flea – size, diet, ability to fly etc. But the SILLY answer is:

> A dog can have fleas,
> but a flea can't have dogs!

Grown-ups don't get this. Ask your dad . . .

> What's the difference
> between a piano and a fish?

. . . and he'll think of all the real differences:

Well, one's a musical instrument, and the other is a vertebrate. And of course, one is edible, whilst the other . . .

Aaaaggghh! Of course the answer is:

> You can tune a piano
> but you can't tuna fish!

'Difference' jokes are great for insulting people.
Ask your sister:

> What's the difference between
> you and a sunset?
> Sunsets are beautiful!

> What's the difference between
> you and a boring TV show?
> You can switch off a boring TV show!

'Difference' jokes are really good for performing.
Here's one to try on your friends.

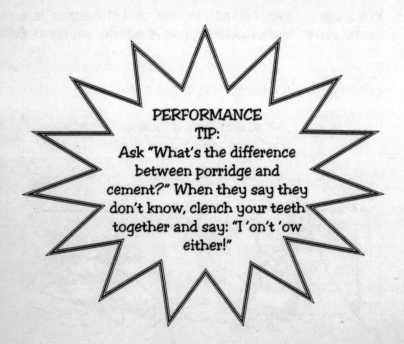

PERFORMANCE
TIP:
Ask "What's the difference
between porridge and
cement?" When they say they
don't know, clench your teeth
together and say: "I 'on't 'ow
either!"

MAKE YOUR OWN

Draw a line between the feed line and the correct punchline to make 3 whole jokes!

What's the difference between a smelly dog and a dead insect?

One's all grown, the other's all g-r-o-a-n!

What's the difference between an adult and a ghost?

One composed, the other decomposed!

What's the difference between Mozart and a dead witch?

One's a seedy beast, the other's a deceased bee!

YOU CRACKED IT!

What's the difference between a smelly dog and a dead insect?

One's all grown, the other's all g-r-o-a-n!

What's the difference between an adult and a ghost?

One composed, the other decomposed!

What's the difference between Mozart and a dead witch?

One's a seedy beast, the other's a deceased bee!

MAKE YOUR OWN

What's the difference between a snake and a head teacher?

One's a good puzzler, the other's a pud guzzler!

What's the difference between a school bully and school gravy?

You can make a pet out of a snake!

What's the difference between a crossword expert and a greedy boy?

School gravy's only thick some of the time!

YOU CRACKED IT!

What's the difference between a snake and a head teacher?

One's a good puzzler, the other's a pud guzzler!

What's the difference between a school bully and school gravy?

You can make a pet out of a snake!

What's the difference between a crossword expert and a greedy boy?

School gravy's only thick some of the time!

MAKE YOUR OWN

What's the difference between a princess and a fresh loaf?

A hill goes up, and a pill goes down!

What's the difference between a hill and a pill?

One has claws at the end of its paws, the other a pause at the end of a clause!

What's the difference between a tiger and a comma?

One's a well-bred maid, the other's well-made bread!

YOU CRACKED IT!

What's the difference between a princess and a fresh loaf?

A hill goes up, and a pill goes down!

What's the difference between a hill and a pill?

One has claws at the end of its paws, the other a pause at the end of a clause!

What's the difference between a tiger and a comma?

One's a well-bred maid, the other's well-made bread!

NOW MAKE 'EM LAUGH

What's the difference between . . .
dog food and cottage pie?
I don't know.
Then I'm not eating at your house!

What's the difference between . . .
rabbits and hares?
You don't get rabbits in your armpits!

What's the difference between . . .
a teacher with a toothache and a black cloud?
One roars with pain, the other pours with rain!

What's the difference between . . .
Mel B and James Bond's girlfriend?
One's a Spice Girl, the other's a spy's girl!

What's the difference between . . .
A big sister and a book?
You can shut up a book!

What's the difference between . . .
A lemon, a dinosaur and a tube of glue?
I dunno.
You can squeeze a lemon but you can't squeeze a dinosaur!
But what about the glue?
I thought that's where you'd get stuck!

What's the difference between . . .
An African elephant and an Indian elephant?
About 5,000 kilometres!

What's the difference between . . .
A buffalo and a bison?
You can't wash your hands in a buffalo!

What's the difference between . . .
the school bell and a mobile phone?
One rings between lessons, the other rings during
them!

DRING
DRING

What's the difference between . . .
A fly and a bird?
A bird can fly but a fly can't bird!

What's the difference between . . .
A ghost and peanut butter?
A ghost doesn't stick to the roof of your mouth!

What's the difference between . . .
A lazy dog and a lazy pupil?
One rarely bites, the other barely writes!

What's the difference between . . .
A kangaroo and a woodcutter?
One hops and chews, the other chops and hews!

What's the difference between . . .
A bus driver and a large piece of snot?
One knows the stops, the other stops the nose!

What's the difference between . . .
A doornail and a boxer?
One gets knocked in, the other gets knocked out!

What's the difference between . . .
A stationmaster and a chess set?
One minds the trains, the other trains the mind!

What's the difference between . . .
A bad pupil and a fisherman?
One hates books, the other baits hooks!

What's the difference between . . .
A teacher and a train?
One says: "Spit that sweet out!",
the other says: "Choo, choo!"

What's the difference between . . .
A cat that likes mice and whale blubber?
One's a fat lot of good, the other's a good lot of
fat!

What's the difference between . . .
A Brownie and a biscuit?
Have you ever dunked a Brownie in your tea?

What's the difference between . . .
A camel and an older brother?
One's a big, smelly, bad-tempered beast,
the other's an animal that lives in the desert!

What's the difference between . . .
Father Christmas and a hot dog?
Father Christmas wears a jolly red suit,
a hot dog just pants!

What's the difference between . . .
A little brother and a bogey?
A bogey only gets up your nose sometimes!

What's the difference between . . .
School dinners and a heap of woodlice?
School dinners come on a plate!

What's the difference between . . .
A bell-ringer and a rotten banana?
One peals madly, the other peels badly!

What's the difference between . . .
A landlord and a learner driver?
One collects rents, the other collects dents!

What's the difference between . . .
A skunk and a schoolteacher?
A schoolteacher uses cheaper deodorant!

What's the difference between . . .
A photocopier and measles?
One makes facsimiles, the other makes sick
families!

What's the difference between . . .
An angry rabbit and a forged banknote?
One's a mad bunny, the other's bad money!

What's the difference between . . .
porridge and putty?
I dunno.
You're not replacing *my* windows, then!

What's the difference between . . .
A drain and a sewer?
A drain can't make dresses!

Doctor, Doctor!

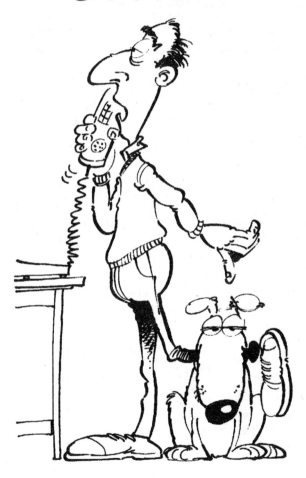

Anyone who's been to the doctor's knows . . .

It's not funny!

You don't go to the doctor for ice cream or to spend your birthday or watch a movie. You go because you're in PAIN!

So why make jokes about it?

There are two main characters in a 'doctor' joke. A mad PATIENT who runs into the surgery with a silly complaint:

"Doctor, Doctor, I think
I'm a snooker ball!"

And a DOCTOR who makes a funny reply:

"Get to the end of the cue!"

In the best 'doctor' jokes, the patient already has something funny wrong with him. This gets you laughing before you've even heard the punchline!

The Doctor usually gets the punchline — but sometimes the patient does:

Patient:
"Doctor, Doctor, I keep losing my memory!"
Doc:
"When did this start?"
Patient:
"When did what start?"

As well as cheering us up, 'doctor' jokes teach us a really important thing: If your doctor has patients like these, change your doctor!

PERFORMANCE
TIP:
Make the patient sound
really mad and out of
breath! And give the
doctor a funny accent.

MAKE YOUR OWN!

Now make your own 'doctor' jokes. Fill in the blanks using some of the words at the bottom of the page.

Doctor, Doctor!
I think I'm turning into a

I'm completely stumped!

Doctor, Doctor!
I've just swallowed a

Don't worry, the change will do you good!

Doctor, Doctor!
Whenever I drink tea I get a terrible pain in my

Try taking the spoon out of the cup!

chicken, eye, coin, knee, cricket bat, pencil

YOU CRACKED IT!

Doctor, Doctor!
I think I'm turning into a

cricket bat!

I'm completely stumped!

Doctor, Doctor!
I've just swallowed a

coin!

Don't worry, the change will do you good!

Doctor, Doctor!
Whenever I drink tea I get a terrible pain in my

eye!

Try taking the spoon out of the cup!

MAKE YOUR OWN!

Doctor, Doctor!
I feel like a

[   ]

Well, I'll be darned!

Doctor, Doctor!
I think I've died and become a

[   ]

I'm sorry, I can't see you right now!

Doctor, Doctor!
I keep thinking I'm a

[   ]

Perch over there and I'll tweet you in a moment!

ghost, apple, pencil, canary, motorway, holey sock

YOU CRACKED IT!

Doctor, Doctor!
I feel like a

holey sock!

Well, I'll be darned!

Doctor, Doctor!
I think I've died and become a

ghost!

I'm sorry, I can't see you right now!

Doctor, Doctor!
I keep thinking I'm a

canary!

Perch over there and I'll tweet you in a moment!

MAKE YOUR OWN!

Doctor, Doctor!
Can you give me something for

Why not try this kite?

Doctor, Doctor!
I think I'm turning into a

Don't worry, I won't bite you!

Doctor, Doctor!
I keep thinking I'm a

Take this pill now and I'll ring you later!

doorbell, cooker, shiny red apple, wind,
athlete's foot, cow

YOU CRACKED IT!

Doctor, Doctor!
Can you give me something for

> wind?

Why not try this kite?

Doctor, Doctor!
I think I'm turning into a

> shiny red apple!

Don't worry, I won't bite you!

Doctor, Doctor!
I keep thinking I'm a

> doorbell!

Take this pill now and I'll ring you later!

MAKE YOUR OWN!

Doctor, Doctor!
Last night I dreamed I was a

[_____] and a [_____]

The problem is you're two tents!

Doctor, Doctor!
I feel like a

[_____]

Hang on while I make some notes!

Doctor, Doctor!
I've just swallowed a

[_____]

Sit over there and don't stir!

vampire, piano, egg, wigwam, dog, tepee, teaspoon

YOU CRACKED IT!

Doctor, Doctor!
Last night I dreamed I was a
wigwam and a teepee!

The problem is you're two tents!

Doctor, Doctor!
I feel like a

piano!

Hang on while I make some notes!

Doctor, Doctor!
I've just swallowed a

teaspoon!

Sit over there and don't stir!

NOW MAKE 'EM LAUGH

Doctor, Doctor!
My ears keep ringing.
Change your number!

Doctor, Doctor!
I think I'm a banana!
Well slip over there and peel off your clothes!

Doctor, Doctor!
Yesterday I swallowed a light bulb.
There'll soon be a light at the end of the tunnel.

Doctor, Doctor!
No one ever believes what I say!
Yes they do.

Doctor, Doctor!
I'm feeling terribly run down!
Try looking both ways when you cross the street!

Doctor, Doctor!
Do you have anything for my liver!
Of course. Here's some bacon and gravy.

Doctor, Doctor!
I think I've turned into an ugly duckling!
I'm not some quack, you know!

Doctor, Doctor!
I keep thinking I'm a refrigerator.
Close your mouth, the little light's shining in my
eyes!

Doctor, Doctor!
I need to lose about 15 kilos!
Well put your shopping down for a start!

Doctor, Doctor!
I've lost my memory!
Well, if you'd just pay the £12,000 you owe me,
I'll do what I can!

Doctor, Doctor!
I've got small blue flowers growing between my
toes!
Don't worry, they're just cornflowers!

Doctor, Doctor!
I keep having dizzy spells!
When do they start?
Every time I step off the roundabout!

Doctor, Doctor!
I've gone blind! Whatever shall I do?
Put your crash helmet on the right way round!

Doctor, Doctor!
I can't stop sneezing. What can you give me?
A tissue?
Oh no, it's happening to you as well!

Doctor, Doctor!
I'm turning into a giant eel. What shall I do?
Don't worry, there's no charge!

Doctor, Doctor!
I think I'm a pack of cards!
Don't worry I'll deal with it!

Doctor, Doctor!
My wife thinks she's a motorbike!
Give her this medicine and she'll get better.
Then how will I get home?

Doctor, Doctor!
I've only got one tooth left. What should I do?
You'll just have to grin and bare it!

Doctor, Doctor!
I think I'm turning into a sweater!
Well pull over, and let's have a look at you!

Doctor, Doctor!
My corn's something awful!
Spread this ointment on it.
What — all over the field?

Doctor, Doctor!
I think I'm about to lay an egg!
Don't count your chickens before they hatch.

Doctor, Doctor!
Do you think I'm turning into a shark?
No, there's no fin to worry about!

Doctor, Doctor!
I think I've swallowed my recorder!
Just be glad you don't play the piano!

Doctor, Doctor!
My boyfriend's hand isn't connected to his
shoulder.
What should I do?
I'd give him the elbow!

Doctor, Doctor!
Do you think I should have a transplant?
We'd better have a good heart-to-heart first!

Doctor, Doctor!
My sister thinks she's a seabird!
She'll just have to wait her tern!

Doctor, Doctor!
I keep thinking I'm a nit!
Just get out of my hair!

Doctor, Doctor!
I'm turning into a chameleon!
I think you're just a little off colour!

Doctor, Doctor!
My face is dead white, and my nose is bright red!
What shall I do?
Stop clowning around!

Doctor, Doctor!
I'm turning into a giant ostrich!
You could have knocked me down with a feather!

Doctor, Doctor!
I think I'm a hungry puppy!
You're pulling my leg!

Doctor, Doctor!
My wife says I'm overweight, unshaven and out all
night!
That's between you and your wife, Santa!

If You Cross . . . !

⇨
Select **IF YOU CROSS . . .**

🤖🤖 2 very different things!

⊸ "What do you get if you cross
a _____ with a _____?"

🐦 A funny way of mixing them up!

People keep mixing strange things together!

Like bananas and toffee in BANOFFEE PIE!

But what do you get if you mix a snake with a Lego set?

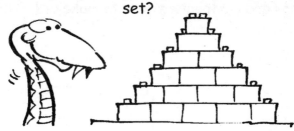

A Boa Constructor!

The question "What do you get if you cross . . . " makes you SMILE because you can't imagine what you'd end up with!

The punchline hits you with the big LAUGH because it mixes the two things together in a funny way.

'Cross' jokes make us look at the world differently. Artists mix different things together to make us THINK:

Advertisers mix things together to make us BUY
things and cartoonists do it to make us LAUGH!

PERFORMANCE
TIP:
Use your hands to tell a
joke, e.g. "What do you get if
you cross a bird (*raise left hand*)
with a frog?" (*raise right hand*)
"Pigeon toed!" (*put hands
together in a clap!*)

MAKE YOUR OWN

Now make your own 'cross' jokes. Fill in the blanks using the words at the bottom of each page!

WHAT DO YOU GET IF YOU CROSS . . .

[ ] WITH [ ] ?

A HEN THAT LAYS TABLES (ouch)!

WHAT DO YOU GET IF YOU CROSS . . .

[ ] WITH [ ] ?

A WALKIE-TALKIE!

WHAT DO YOU GET IF YOU CROSS . . .

[ ] WITH [ ] ?

A BITE IN SHINING ARMOUR!

a parrot, a waiter, a mosquito, a centipede,
a chicken, a knight

YOU *CRACKED* IT!

WHAT DO YOU GET IF YOU CROSS...

a waiter   WITH   a chicken   ?

A HEN THAT LAYS TABLES (ouch)!

WHAT DO YOU GET IF YOU CROSS...

a parrot   WITH   a centipede   ?

A WALKIE-TALKIE!

WHAT DO YOU GET IF YOU CROSS...

a mosquito   WITH   a knight   ?

A BITE IN SHINING ARMOUR!

CHOMP!!

MAKE YOUR OWN

WHAT DO YOU GET IF YOU CROSS . . .

(_____) WITH (_____) ?

SANTA CLAWS!

WHAT DO YOU GET IF YOU CROSS . . .

(_____) WITH (_____) ?

A WOMBAT!

WHAT DO YOU GET IF YOU CROSS . . .

(_____) WITH (_____) ?

ASTON VANILLA!

a football team, a leopard, a bat, an ice cream,
Father Christmas, a Womble

YOU CRACKED IT!

WHAT DO YOU GET IF YOU CROSS . . .

| Father Christmas | WITH | a leopard | ?

SANTA CLAWS!

WHAT DO YOU GET IF YOU CROSS . . .

| a Womble | WITH | a bat | ?

A WOMBAT!

WHAT DO YOU GET IF YOU CROSS . . .

| a football team | WITH | an ice cream | ?

ASTON VANILLA!

MAKE YOUR OWN

WHAT DO YOU GET IF YOU CROSS . . .

( ) WITH ( ) ?

A HUMBURGER!

WHAT DO YOU GET IF YOU CROSS . . .

( ) WITH ( ) ?

FROSTBITE!

WHAT DO YOU GET IF YOU CROSS . . .

( ) WITH ( ) ?

PEELS OF LAUGHTER!

a vampire, a quarter-pounder, a snowman, an
orange, a bee, a comedian

YOU CRACKED IT!

WHAT DO YOU GET IF YOU CROSS...

| a bee | WITH | a quarter-pounder | ?

A HUMBURGER!

WHAT DO YOU GET IF YOU CROSS...

| a snowman | WITH | a vampire | ?

FROSTBITE!

WHAT DO YOU GET IF YOU CROSS...

| an orange | WITH | a comedian | ?

PEELS OF LAUGHTER!

MAKE YOUR OWN

WHAT DO YOU GET IF YOU CROSS . . .

(⬚) WITH (⬚) ?

SHERLOCK BONES!

WHAT DO YOU GET IF YOU CROSS . . .

(⬚) WITH (⬚) ?

A COLD SPELL!

WHAT DO YOU GET IF YOU CROSS . . .

(⬚) WITH (⬚) ?

A HARDENED CRIMINAL!

a concrete mixer, a skeleton, a witch, a burglar,
an ice cube, a detective

YOU CRACKED IT!

WHAT DO YOU GET IF YOU CROSS ...

| a detective | WITH | a skeleton | ?

SHERLOCK BONES!

WHAT DO YOU GET IF YOU CROSS ...

| an ice cube | WITH | a witch | ?

A COLD SPELL!

WHAT DO YOU GET IF YOU CROSS ...

| a concrete mixer | WITH | a burglar | ?

A HARDENED CRIMINAL!

MAKE YOUR OWN

WHAT DO YOU GET IF YOU CROSS . . .

(_____) WITH (_____) ?

A SNACK THAT GOES CRUNCH IN THE NIGHT!

WHAT DO YOU GET IF YOU CROSS . . .

(_____) WITH (_____) ?

ROOST BEEF!

WHAT DO YOU GET IF YOU CROSS . . .

(_____) WITH (_____) ?

A RAT-A-TAT-TAT!

a rat, a chicken, a ghost, a packet of crisps,
a woodpecker, a cow

YOU CRACKED IT!

WHAT DO YOU GET IF YOU CROSS . . .

a ghost   WITH   a packet of crisps ?

A SNACK THAT GOES CRUNCH IN THE NIGHT!

WHAT DO YOU GET IF YOU CROSS . . .

a chicken   WITH   a cow ?

ROOST BEEF!

WHAT DO YOU GET IF YOU CROSS . . .

a rat   WITH   a woodpecker ?

A RAT-A-TAT-TAT!

NOW MAKE 'EM LAUGH

What do you get if you cross . . .
a zookeeper with a teacher?
Someone who gives you 100 lions for being late!

What do you get if you cross . . .
a frog with a fizzy drink?
A can of croak!

What do you get if you cross . . .
a collie with an Alsatian?
A dog that rounds up criminals!

What do you get if you cross . . .
a railway line with a tortoise?
Run over!

What do you get if you cross . . .
a snake with a wizard?
An Abrada-cobra!

What do you get if you cross . . .
a serpent with a trumpet?
A snake in the brass!

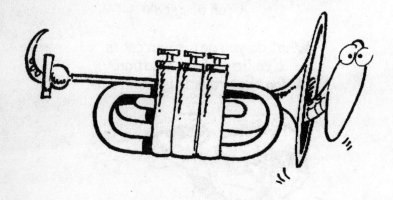

What do you get if you cross . . .
a python with a glow-worm?
A 20-foot strip light!

What do you get if you cross . . .
a glow-worm with a pint of beer?
Light ale!

What do you get if you cross . . .
a muppet with a dress shop?
Kermit the Frock!

What do you get if you cross . . .
a crab with a cactus?
Pinch and needles!

What do you get if you cross . . .
a snowman with a crocodile?
Frostbite!

What do you get if you cross . . .
a pig with a centipede?
Bacon and leggs!

What do you get if you cross . . .
a romantic hero with a school janitor?
Someone who sweeps you off your feet!

What do you get if you cross . . .
a very old chicken with a very young chicken?
A Henbryo!

What do you get if you cross . . .
a sheepdog with a plate of jelly?
The collie-wobbles!

What do you get if you cross . . .
a broomstick with a policeman?
A brush with the law!

What do you get if you cross . . .
a skunk with a dumb owl?
A creature that smells but doesn't give a hoot!

What do you get if you cross . . .
a joke book with an Oxo cube?
A laughing stock!

What do you get if you cross . . .
a bee with a gorilla?
Sting Kong!

What do you get if you cross . . .
a trumpet, a piano with a rubber?
An elastic band!

What do you get if you cross . . .
an elephant with a canary?
A messy cage!

What do you get if you cross . . .
an elephant with a kangaroo?
Big holes all over Australia!

What do you get if you cross . . .
a kangaroo with a mouse?
Big holes in your cheese!

What do you get if you cross . . .
a kangaroo with a yeti?
A fur coat with big pockets!

What do you get if you cross . . .
a cat with a parrot?
A carrot!

What do you get if you cross . . .
a cat with a tree?
A catalog!

What do you get if you cross . . .
a cat with a bottle of vinegar?
A sourpuss!

What do you get if you cross . . .
a cat with a gorilla?
An animal that puts *you* out at night!

What do you get if you cross . . .
A werewolf with a hyena?
I don't know — but if it laughs, join in!

What do you get if you cross . . .
the Atlantic with the Titanic?
Halfway!

What do you get if you cross . . .
A mummy with a mechanic?
Toot and Carman!

Knock, Knock!

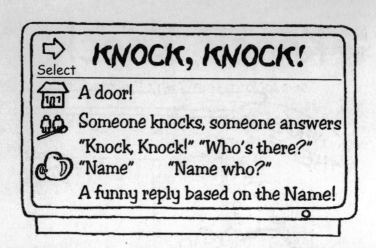

In 'Knock, Knock' jokes there are two people either side of a DOOR:

Knock, Knock!   Who's there?

The person knocking replies, giving an ordinary NAME:

Doris who?

Now the 'name' turns magically into the start of a sentence:

Doris locked, that's why I'm knocking!

Most 'Knock, Knock' jokes are puns on someone's name. There are so many, why not make them up using your friends' names!

You can also use food, animals, clothes . . . anything you like!

Knock, Knock!
Who's there?
Jewel.
Jewel who?
Jewel know in a sec!

Wooden shoe.
Wooden shoe who?
Wooden shoe like to know!

"Knock, Knock" was the catchphrase of a comedian called Wee George Wood. But the jokes started in Victorian times.

Kids sat in a circle. One of them bashed a stick on the floor.

Knock, Knock!

Buff.

Who's there?

What says Buff?

If the kid with the stick made Buff laugh or smile, Buff kept the stick and tried the rhyme on someone else. Not funny today, but it started the idea of 'Knock, Knock' jokes!

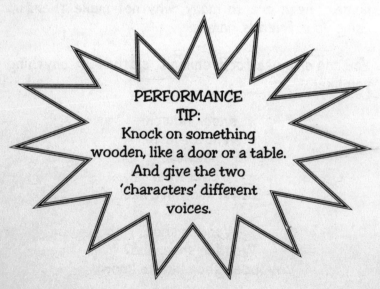

PERFORMANCE TIP:
Knock on something wooden, like a door or a table. And give the two 'characters' different voices.

MAKE YOUR OWN!

Make your own 'Knock, Knock' jokes. Each PUNCHLINE is missing, so use the 'name' to help you think one up. Then compare your jokes to the ones on the next page!

Knock, Knock!
Who's there?
Ivor.
Ivor who?

Ivor

Knock, Knock!
Who's there?
Neil.
Neil who?

Neil

Knock, Knock!
Who's there?
Turner.
Turner who?

Turner

YOU CRACKED IT!

Here are our punchlines — bet yours are better!

Knock, Knock!
Who's there?
Ivor.
Ivor who?

Ivor great idea!

Knock, Knock!
Who's there?
Neil.
Neil who?

Neil down and look through the letter box!

Knock, Knock!
Who's there?
Turner.
Turner who?

Turner round, there's a monster behind you!

MAKE YOUR OWN!

Knock, Knock!
Who's there?
Annette.
Annette who?

Annette

Knock, Knock!
Who's there?
Canoe.
Canoe who?

Canoe

Knock, Knock!
Who's there?
Scold.
Scold who?

Scold

I DON'T KNOW !! STREWTH, IT'S COLD OUT HERE !

YOU CRACKED IT!

Here are our punchlines — bet yours are better!

Knock, Knock!
Who's there?
Annette.
Annette who?

Annette is good for fishing!

Knock, Knock!
Who's there?
Canoe.
Canoe who?

Canoe open the door, please?

Knock, Knock!
Who's there?
Scold.
Scold who?

Scold out here!

MAKE YOUR OWN!

Knock, Knock!
Who's there?
Mary.
Mary who?

Mary

Knock, Knock!
Who's there?
Howard.
Howard who?

Howard

Knock, Knock!
Who's there?
Mike.
Mike who?

Mike

MIKE I HAVE THE
PLEASURE OF
THIS DANCE ?

YOU CRACKED IT!

Here are our punchlines — bet yours are better!

Knock, Knock!
Who's there?
Mary.
Mary who?

Mary Christmas to you!

Knock, Knock!
Who's there?
Howard.
Howard who?

Howard you like to go to the cinema?

Knock, Knock!
Who's there?
Mike.
Mike who?

Mike car is parked over there!

NOW MAKE 'EM LAUGH

Knock, Knock!
Who's there?
Yorkie.
Yorkie who?
Yorkie is still in the door!

Knock, Knock!
Who's there?
Des.
Des who?
Des a parcel for you!

Knock, Knock!
Who's there?
Simon.
Simon who?
Simon the door says 'Room to Let'.

Knock, Knock!
Who's there?
Grant.
Grant who?
Well, er, it's Hugh Grant actually, sorry, er . . .

Knock, Knock!
Who's there?
Cricket.
Cricket who?
Cricket neck so I can't bend over!

Knock, Knock!
Who's there?
Owl.
Owl who?
Owl be sad if you don't answer!

Knock, Knock!
Who's there?
Missy.
Missy who?
I miss you too!

Knock, Knock!
Who's there?
June.
June who?
June know there's a dog on your doorstep?

Knock, Knock!
Who's there?
Jason.
Jason who?
Jason around is very tiring!

Knock, Knock!
Who's there?
Lettuce.
Lettuce who?
Lettuce go to the swings!

Knock, Knock!
Who's there?
Boo.
Boo who?
Don't cry!

Knock, Knock!
Who's there?
Jackson.
Jackson who?
Jackson holiday, but I'm here!

Knock, Knock!
Who's there?
Sadie.
Sadie who?
Sadie magic words!

Knock, Knock!
Who's there?
Kenny.
Kenny who?
Kenny have his ball back?

Knock, Knock!
Who's there?
Aladdin.
Aladdin who?
Aladdin need of somewhere to stay!

Knock, Knock!
Who's there?
Rice.
Rice who?
Rice you to the end of the road!

Knock, Knock!
Who's there?
Triumph.
Triumph who?
Triumph, he lives across the street!

Knock, Knock!
Who's there?
Twitter Twitter.
Twitter Twitter who?
I didn't know you had an owl!

Knock, Knock!
Who's there?
A niggle.
A niggle who?
No it's a bungalow!

Knock, Knock!
Who's there?
Julie.
Julie who?
Julie va message on my answerphone?

Knock, Knock!
Who's there?
Kipper.
Kipper who?
Kipper your hands in the air!

Knock, Knock!
Who's there?
Duke.
Duke who?
Duke come here often?

Knock, Knock!
Who's there?
Uncle Pete.
Uncle Pete who?
How many Uncle Petes have you got?

Knock, Knock!
Who's there?
Othello.
Othello who?
Othello could grow old
waiting for you to answer the door!

Knock, Knock!
Who's there?
Mandy.
Mandy who?
Mandy muck on the doormat . . . too late!

Knock, Knock!
Who's there?
Alf.
Alf who?
Alf fetch a ladder, you're snowed in!

Knock, Knock!
Who's there?
How dude!
How dude who?
Very well, thanks!

Knock ,Knock!
Who's there?
Annakin.
Annakin who?
Annakin reach the doorbell, but I have to knock!

Knock, Knock!
Who's there?
Guess.
Guess who?
I know who you are, who am I?

Knock, Knock!
Who's there?
Jelly.
Jelly who?
Jelly've your light on all night?

Knock, Knock!
Who's there?
Hide.
Hide who?
Then I proclaim us husband and wife!

Knock, Knock!
Who's there?
Nova.
Nova who?
No varnish on your front door, it'll warp!

Light bulbs!

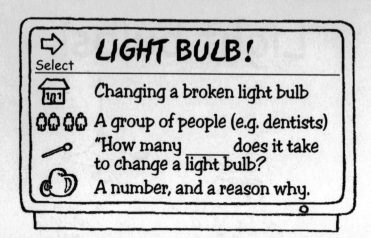

Question: What's funny about this picture?

OK, there's nothing funny about changing a light bulb! But you can TEASE different groups by describing HOW they would change it.

How many jugglers does it
take to change a light bulb?
Only one: but it takes a lot of bulbs!

Another group you can make fun of are head teachers:

How many head teachers does it
take to change a light bulb?
Two! One to call the caretaker,
the other to blame the kids!

OK, not all head teachers are lazy — or blame the kids when something gets broken. But it's funny all the same.

'Light bulb' jokes can be about any group you like:

Teachers	Doctors	Football managers
Dinosaurs	Golfers	Tree surgeons
Cartoonists	Vets	Ice-cream sellers
FBI agents	Builders	Pop Stars
Conjurors	Ghosts	Mummies

PERFORMANCE
TIP:
Do the punchline in the
'voice' of the people you're
making fun of: e.g. 'bossy' head
teacher, 'croaky' grandparent,
'posh' Queen, 'spooky'
vampire.

MAKE YOUR OWN

Now make your own 'light bulb' jokes! Fill in the blanks using *some* of the words at the bottom of the page.

How many ⬚⬚⬚⬚⬚⬚⬚ does it take
to change a light bulb?
Two! One to screw in the bulb,
the other to pull the ladder away!

How many ⬚⬚⬚⬚⬚⬚⬚ does it take
to change a light bulb?
Two! One to remove the rotten bulb,
the other to fill in the cavity!

How many ⬚⬚⬚⬚⬚⬚⬚ does it take
to change a light bulb?
Only one, but it's definitely a change for the
'better'!

*gamblers, soldiers, dentists, elephants, school
bullies*

YOU CRACKED IT!

How many (school bullies) does it take
to change a light bulb?
Two! One to screw in the bulb,
the other to pull the ladder away!

How many (dentists) does it take
to change a light bulb?
Two! One to remove the rotten bulb,
the other to fill in the cavity!

How man (gamblers) does it take
to change a light bulb?
Only one, but it's definitely a change for the
'better'

MAKE YOUR OWN!

As before, fill in the blanks using *some* of the words at the bottom of the page.

How many ⬚ does it take
to change a light bulb?
None! They're all bone idle!

How many ⬚ does it take
to change a light bulb?
Only one, but watch out – she'll change it into a toad!

How many ⬚ does it take
to change a light bulb?
Two! One to screw in the new bulb,
the other to turn the old bulb into something useful!

Wombles, frogs, skeletons, sailors, witches

YOU CRACKED IT!

How many (skeletons) does it take
to change a light bulb?
None! They're all bone idle!

How many (witches) does it take
to change a light bulb?
Only one, but watch out — she'll change it into a
toad!

How many (Wombles) does it take
to change a light bulb?
Two! One to screw in the new bulb,
the other to turn the old bulb into something
useful!

NOW MAKE 'EM LAUGH

How many magicians
does it take to change a light bulb?
Depends what you want it changed into!

How many grandparents
does it take to change a light bulb?
Two! One to screw the new one in, the other
to tell you how much better the old one was!

How many Blue Peter presenters
does it take to change a light bulb?
Two! One to put in a new bulb,
the other to turn the old one
into a Xmas decoration!

How many old Jedi Knights
does it take to change a light bulb?
Obi Wan!
(only one)

How many clever teachers
does it take to change a light bulb?
Both of them!

How many fishermen
does it take to change a light bulb?
Only one — but you should have seen
the size of the bulb, it was this big!

How many dinosaurs
does it take to change a light bulb?
None — they didn't have light bulbs then!

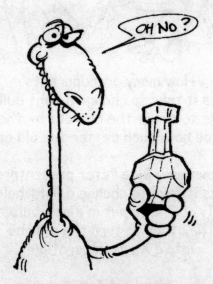

How many cells
does it take to change a light bulb?
One. No, two. No, four.
Eight. Sixteen, thirty-two . . .

How many fire fighters
does it take to change a light bulb?
Four! Three to cut a hole in the roof,
and one to screw in the bulb!

How many monsters
does it take to change a light bulb?
Three! Two to screw in the new bulb,
one to eat the old one!

How many stupid people
does it take to change a light bulb?
Ten! One to screw in the bulb,
nine to find the matches!

How many magpies
does it take to change a light bulb?
One . . . for sorrow, two for joy,
three for a girl, four for a boy!

How many vampires
does it take to change a light bulb?
None! They like the dark!

How many Premier League footballers
does it take to change a light bulb?
Ask my manager, he arranges transfers!

How many parents
does it take to change a light bulb?
We'll see.

How many Martians
does it take to change a light bulb?
Two and a half!

One!
How many mind-readers
does it take to change a light bulb?

How many farmers
does it take to change a light bulb?
Only one — if he remembers where he planted it!

How many Queens of England
does it take to change a light bulb?
One . . . gets the butler to do it!

How many stupid people
does it take to change a light bulb?
One! But it has to be a very dim bulb!

How many light bulbs
does it take to change a light bulb?
Watts and watts!

How many Klingons
does it take to change a light bulb?
Only one — but three others must
die fighting for the honour!

How many Fox Mulders
does it take to change a light bulb?
You see a light bulb,
I see an alien artefact!

How many transplant surgeons
does it take to change a light bulb?
Two! One to make an incision in the glass,
the other to insert the donor filament!

Laughter!

Just about everybody in the world laughs — at least once in their lives. But what exactly IS laughter?

LAUGHTER . . .

. . . is something only humans do!

LAUGHTER . . .

. . . helps us to release extra energy or tension!

LAUGHTER . . .

. . . uses 44 muscles and 2 bones but *not* the funny bone!

LAUGHTER . . .

. . . is extremely infectious!

LAUGHTER . . .

. . . is also good for your health!

LAUGHTER . . .

. . . comes in all shapes and sizes!

GIGGLE TITTER!

CHUCKLE

SNIGGER

SNORT! HOWL

HOOT

CACKLE SPLITS
WHOOP YOUR
DOUBLE UP SIDES
FALL ABOUT

Limericks!

A limerick is a story told in five rhyming lines.
There are all sorts but most of them work like this.

Line 1 . . .
introduces a *character* from somewhere:

There was a young man from *Belize*

Line 2 . . .
rhymes with Line 1:

Who went to the doc with a *sneeze*

Lines 3 & 4 . . .
rhyme together and say what happened:

The doc added a *hose*

To the young man's sore *nose*

Line 5 . . .
rhymes with Lines 1 & 2 and is the PUNCHLINE:

Now his snot's in the South China *Seas*!

Limericks nearly always rhyme but sometimes it's funny if they don't. This one looks like it rhymes — but when you read it, it doesn't rhyme at all!

A man with a terrible cough
Walked straight through a window in Slough
He said later: "Although
It was terribly rough,
There are worse things I could have gone through!"

Limericks were invented by a very funny poet called Edward Lear, who wrote lots of nonsense verses.

But WHY are they called 'limericks'?
Limerick is a place in Ireland.
And as we all know, the Irish are brilliant at jokes!

Limericks may have started with a Victorian game. Five party-goers would make up a story, taking turns to do a line:

A group of five friends from Dundee
Held a limerick party to see
Whose rhyme was the best
–And when put to the test
The winner got fruitcake for tea!

When they finished, they would all chant:

"Will you come up to Limerick?"

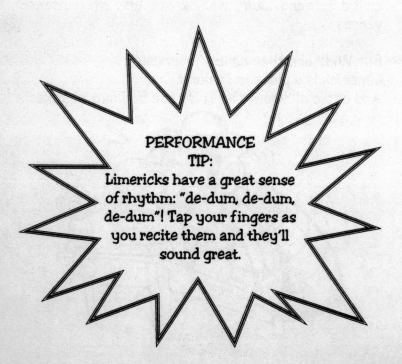

PERFORMANCE
TIP:
Limericks have a great sense
of rhythm: "de-dum, de-dum,
de-dum"! Tap your fingers as
you recite them and they'll
sound great.

MAKE YOUR OWN

Use *THREE* of the rhyming words in the circle to help you finish the limerick. Then compare it to the limerick on the next page!

A mathematician called ⬚,

Is the worst adder-upper ⬚.

When all he must do
Is to add 2 and 2,

He still makes the sum come to ⬚!

YOU CRACKED IT!

A mathematician called CLIVE

Is the worst adder-upper ALIVE.

When all he must do
Is to add 2 and 2,

He still makes the sum come to FIVE!

MAKE YOUR OWN

Use *THREE* of the rhyming words in the circle to help you finish the limerick. Then compare it to the limerick on the next page!

There was a young lady from ⬚ ,

Who was terribly tidy and ⬚ .

As she got out of bed
She would stand on her head,

To avoid getting dirt on her ⬚ !

BEAT CRETE NEAT
FEET HEAT WHEAT

YOU CRACKED IT!

There was a young lady from CRETE,

Who was terribly tidy and NEAT.

As she got out of bed
She would stand on her head,

To avoid getting dirt on her FEET!

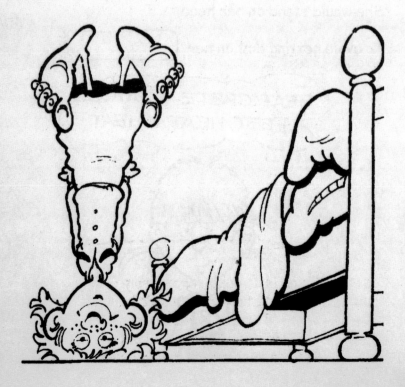

NOW MAKE 'EM LAUGH

There was a young lady from Luton,
Who purchased a Japanese futon,
Each night she retired
Most oddly attired
With a shirt, and a tie, and a suit on!

A little she-vampire called Ruth
Got terrible pains in her tooth
She pulled out the thing
With a door and some string
Now thickth of the otherth are looth!

There is a young fellow from Ghana
Who skateboards upon a banana
To people who scoff
He says: "Yes, I fall off,
But it's easier than riding a llama!"

An African parrot called Scott
Had a beak like the front of a yacht.
I fed him some ham and
He sneezed like a cannon,
And covered my sister in . . . embarrassment!

There was an old lady from Hyde
Who ate so many apples, she died!
The apples fermented
Inside the lamented
And made cider inside her inside!

There was a young man from Bengal
Who was asked to a fancy-dress ball.
He said he would risk it,
And went as a biscuit,
And a dog ate him up in the hall!

There was an old man from Penzance
Who always wore full-metal pants.
He said, "Some years back,
I sat down on a tack,
And I'll never again take a chance!"

There was a young lady from Wales
Who used to bite chimpanzees' nails.
She said, as she chewed:
"Yes, I know that it's rude,
But it's better than biting their tails!"

There was a young man from Quebec
Who wrapped both his legs round his neck.
But then he forgot
How to undo the knot,
And now he's an absolute wreck!

There was a young fellow from Leeds
Who swallowed a packet of seeds.
Within just one hour
His nose was a flower
And his head was a riot of weeds!

There was a young Frenchman from Gaul
Who was terribly, terribly tall.
While lying in bed
He reached out his leg
And turned off the light in the hall!

An admirable butler called Crichton
Spent a week at the seaside near Brighton.
Each day, for a lark
He'd dress up as a shark,
And wait for some bathers to frighten!

Johann Sebastian Bach
Was once overheard to remark:
"I do my composing
Stark naked while dozing
Alone, in the bath, in the dark!"

There was an old man from Vancouver,
Whose wife got sucked into the hoover.
He said: "There's some doubt
If she's more in than out,
But whichever it is, I can't move her!"

There was a young lady called Sue
Who carried a frog in each shoe.
When asked to stop
She replied with a hop:
"But I'm trying to get into *Who's Zoo!*"

There was a young student from Crete,
Who stood on his head in the street.
Said he: "It is clear,
If I mean to stop here,
I shall have to shake hands with my feet!"

A young snooker player called Todd
Played the game in a style that was odd.
He would pick up his cue
And snap it in two,
And then pocket the balls with a cod.

There was an old man from Peru,
Who dreamt he was eating his shoe.
He awoke in the night
In a terrible fright,
And found it was perfectly true!

There was a dead man in a hearse
Who said: "Well, it might have been worse.
Of course the expense
Is simply immense,
But it doesn't come out of *my* purse!"

The fully-grown female Wall-aby
Has a pouch on the front for its baby.
The newborn lives here
For up to a year;
And then it comes out again – maybe!

A lovely young lady called Grace
Had a blooming great zit on her face.
She sighed: "It's so simple
To lose a small pimple,
But this blemish I cannot misplace!"

An overweight fellow called Skinner
Said: "How I wish I was thinner!"
So he lived for six weeks
On one grape and two leeks –
We think of him, sometimes, at dinner!

I once asked a captain called Kirk
To say what he enjoyed in his work.
"No traffic, no queues,
No rain, no bad news,
And no cabbage," he said, with a smirk!

There was a young lady called Hannah
Who slipped on a peel of banana.
She wanted to swear,
But her mother was there,
So she whistled "The Star-spangled Banner".

Mummy, Mummy!

Mummy, Mummy!
Why does next door's cat keep coming round?
It's on a spin cycle!

We all know that mums are wonderful, kind, cuddly people who loves us to bits and never get cross.

Well, this one isn't! Ladies and Gentlemen, meet . . .

THE WORST MUM IN THE WORLD!

In 'Mummy, Mummy' jokes, the mother is a complete disaster. She's mean, rude, greedy, deceitful, selfish . . . and incredibly LAZY.

Mummy, Mummy!
I've grown two inches since Xmas!
Great! Soon, you'll be able to reach the washing-up!

Mind you, the kid in the jokes is a bit of a pain. You can just SEE the kid tugging on the mother's sleeve, and HEAR that whingey, whiny voice going . . .

Mummy, Mummy!
Can I have some sweets?
Oh please, please, please, please, please, please, please, please, please, please, please, please, please, please, please, please, please!

Like many jokes, 'Mummy, Mummy' jokes are funny because we've ALL whinged at our mums at some time, and we've ALL deserved a nasty reply . . .

. . . even if your mum's too nice to say it!

The 'Mummy' isn't just mean to the kid in the jokes
— she's mean to everybody!

Mummy, Mummy!
Daddy's on the line!
And he's staying there until he's completely dry!

PERFORMANCE
TIP:
Give the kid a high
pitched whiny voice, and
give the mum a deep
growl!

MAKE YOUR OWN

Draw a line between the feed line and the correct punchline to make 3 whole jokes!

Mummy, Mummy! The kids at school say you're a witch!

Great! Whose ankle was it?

Mummy, Mummy! I twisted an ankle in the playground!

Dragons? Nonsense! They're zombies. Dragons live under your bed.

Mummy, Mummy! Sarah says there are dragons in the cracks in the pavement!

Shut up or I'll turn you into a toad!

YOU CRACKED IT!

Mummy, Mummy! The kids at school say you're a witch!

Great! Whose ankle was it?

Mummy, Mummy! I twisted an ankle in the playground!

Dragons? Nonsense! They're zombies. Dragons live under your bed.

Mummy, Mummy! Sarah says there are dragons in the cracks in the pavement!

Shut up or I'll turn you into a toad!

MAKE YOUR OWN

Mummy, Mummy! Can I have a puppy!

Tiddlywinks!

Mummy, Mummy! Our teacher said ghosts are everywhere!

Of course, darling. What flavour?

Mummy, Mummy! My music teacher gave me a recorder. What shall I play?

Well, they're not. They're just in the loo and your wardrobe — and only at night.

YOU CRACKED IT!

Mummy, Mummy! Can I have a puppy!

Tiddlywinks!

Mummy, Mummy! Our teacher said ghosts are everywhere!

Of course, darling. What flavour?

Mummy, Mummy! My music teacher gave me a recorder. What shall I play?

Well, they're not. They're just in the loo and your wardrobe – and only at night.

NOW MAKE 'EM LAUGH

Mummy, Mummy!
Can Sarah come round?
How long has she been unconscious?

Mummy, Mummy!
Why are your hands so soft?
Because the servants do the washing-up!

Mummy, Mummy!
Have you seen my wormery?
Be quiet, and eat your spaghetti!

Mummy, Mummy!
What am I getting for my birthday?
A year older!

Mummy, Mummy!
I keep walking round in circles.
Shut up or I'll glue your other foot to the floor!

Mummy, Mummy!
Can I go on the school trip?
Yes.
I thought you said you couldn't afford it?
I bought you a one-way ticket!

Mummy, Mummy!
Can I have a new pair of trainers?
As soon as your brother grows out of them!

Mummy, Mummy!
Are we nearly there yet?
Shut up and keep pedalling!

Mummy, Mummy!
I'm starving!
But now your uniform fits again!

Mummy, Mummy!
My teacher says I've got an inferiority complex.
Hmm. It's not a very big one, is it?

Mummy, Mummy!
My arm hurts!
Stop waving the aerial about, the TV's gone fuzzy!

Mummy, Mummy!
This turkey isn't cooked properly.
Sshh. You'll wake him up!

Mummy, Mummy!
Can I have a mobile phone?
Of course. I'll just rip it out of the wall for you!

Mummy, Mummy!
What shall I do when I grow up?
Move!

Mummy, Mummy!
What's for dinner?
Chicken soup.
Mummy, Mummy, I've got a nosebleed!
Correction — tomato soup!

Mummy, Mummy!
When I grow up I want to be like Cinderella.
You can start by scrubbing the floor.

Mummy, Mummy!
Can I have a three-course dinner?
Of course, darling. Here are two chips and a pea.

Mummy, Mummy!
Can I play with grandma?
You've dug her up four times already!

Mummy, Mummy!
Why do I have to tidy my bedroom?
Lodgers are fussy people!

Mummy, Mummy!
Kids at school call me a werewolf!
Shut up and comb your face!

... On The Head!

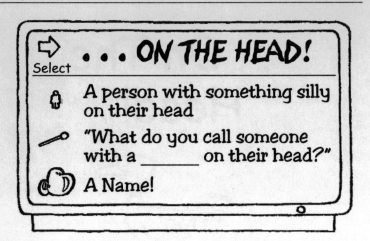

What do you call a man
with a chicken on his head?

HENry!

I have a young friend called Alex. It's easy to make
him laugh. Just say: "A man with a chicken on his
head"!

He's never heard the rest of the joke! He just
pictures a chicken sitting on a man's head and
starts to giggle.

So 'on the head' jokes conjure up a funny picture. They are also about people's NAMES.

Any name that means something else too can work. Take the name 'Bill':

> What do you call a man
> with a duck on his head?
> Bill!

A 'bill' is the mouth of a duck. And a 'bill' can also be a demand for money:

> What do you call a man
> with a brown envelope on his head?
> Bill!

Even nicknames work fine:

> What do you call a man
> with a safe on his head?
> Shorty!

And some of the best ones work in pairs:

What do you call a man
with a spade on his head?

Doug!

What do you call a man
without a spade on his head?

Douglas!

PERFORMANCE
TIP:
'On the head' jokes work
best if you tell 3 or 4 in a
row, ending with a 'pair'
like Doug/Douglas.

MAKE YOUR OWN!

Can you spot a punchine? Have a go below! Match each feed line to ONE of the punchlines. Then turn the page and see if you were a right comedian!

What do you call a boy
with a wig on his head?

AARON
ADAM
ALAN

What do you call a girl
with a kebab on her head?

DAISY
DEBBIE
DONNA

What do you call a boy
with a sheepskin on his head?

SIMON
SHAUN
STEVEN

YOU CRACKED IT!

What do you call a boy
with a wig on his head?

AARON!

What do you call a girl
with a kebab on her head?

DONNA!

What do you call a boy
with a sheepskin on his head?

SHAUN!

MAKE YOUR OWN!

What do you call a girl
with a parrot on her head?

DOLLY
MOLLY
POLLY

What do you call a boy
with bait on his head?

ROD
RON
ROLF

What do you call a woman
with a pyramid on her head?

AUNTIE
SIS
MUMMY

YOU CRACKED IT!

What do you call a girl
with a parrot on her head?

POLLY!

What do you call a boy
with bait on his head?

ROD!

What do you call a woman
with a pyramid on her head?

MUMMY!

MAKE YOUR OWN!

What do you call a girl
with a thorn on her head?

RACHEL
ROSE
RUTH

What do you call a boy
with an aerial on his head?

TEL
TIM
TOM

What do you call a girl
with a frog on her head?

LENA
LILY
LOUISE

YOU CRACKED IT!

What do you call a girl
with a thorn on her head?

ROSE!

What do you call a boy
with an aerial on his head?

TEL!

What do you call a girl
with a frog on her head?

LILY!

MAKE YOUR OWN!

What do you call a girl
with a beach on her head?

SALLY
SANDY
CINDY

What do you call a boy
with a goat on his head?

BENNY
BILLY
BOBBY

What do you call a man
with a bus on his head?

BOSS
SIR
COACH

YOU CRACKED IT!

What do you call a girl
with a beach on her head?

SANDY!

What do you call a boy
with a goat on his head?

BILLY!

What do you call a man
with a bus on his head?

COACH!

NOW MAKE 'EM LAUGH

What do you call a boy
with a rug on his head?
Matt!

What do you call a boy
with a crowbar on his head?
Jimmy!

What do you call a boy
with a Christmas tree on his head?
Noel!

What do you call a boy
with a crown on his head?
King, stupid!

What do you call a girl
with the Tower of Pisa on her head?
Lena!

What do you call a girl
with a basket on her head?
Carrie!

What do you call a girl
with a coin on her head?
Penny!

What do you call a girl
with her *head* on a *coin*?
Queen, stupid!

What do you call a
boy with tiles on his head?
Roofus!

What do you call a boy
with a seagull on his head?
Cliff!

What do you call a boy
with BRIGHTON printed on his head?
Rock!

What do you call a boy
with a lamp on his head?
A miner, stupid!

What do you call a boy
with a crisp packet on his head?
Russell!

What do you call a boy
with a speedometer on his head?
Miles!

What do you call a boy
with a sweatband on his head?
Jim (gym)!

What do you call a boy
with four horses on his head?
Jim Khana!

What do you call a girl
with a Xmas tree on her head?
Holly!

What do you call a girl
with a climber on her head?
Ivy!

What do you call a boy
with a barge on his head?
Derek!

What do you call a girl
with a chocolate bar on her head?
Candy!

What do you call a boy
with a whoopee cushion on his head?
Rudi!

What do you call a boy
with a number plate on his head?
Reg!

What do you call a boy
with a drum on his head?
Tom Tom!

What do you call a boy
with half a drum on his head?
Tom!

What do you call a girl
with the Titanic on her head?
Mandy Lifeboats!

What do you call a boy
with a gardening tool on his head?
Ivanhoe!

What do you call a boy
with a 747 on his head?
Ron Way!

What do you call a girl
with a cash register on her head?
Tilly!

What do you call a girl
with a ball of wool on her head?
Barbara Blacksheep!

What do you call a girl
with a nit on her head?
Alice!

What do you call a boy
with a car on his head?
Jack!

What do you call a boy
with a truck on his head?
Laurie!

What do you call a boy
with Hamlet on his head?
Toby or not Toby!

What do you call a boy
with a bonfire on his head?
Guy!

What do you call a boy
with a lion on his head?
Leo!

What do you call a boy
with a cross lion on his head?
Claude!

What do you call a boy
with a wet biscuit on his head?
Duncan!

What do you call a boy
with a casserole on his head?
Stu Pot!

What do you call a boy
with binoculars on his head?
Luke Closely!

What do you call a girl
with a bow on her head?
Viola!

Stupid!

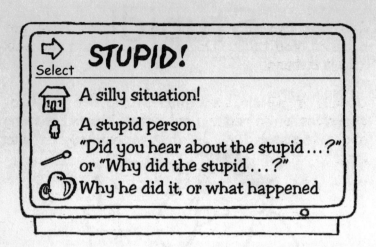

Did you hear about the stupid man
whose phone rang while he was ironing?
He burnt his ear!

We all do stupid things sometimes (Oh yes you do!)
Like:

Putting your trousers on ...
before your pants!

Taking a drink of lemonade ...
and missing!

Getting ready for school ...
in the holidays!

Sending a Valentine ...
to the wrong person!

It's like two wires inside our brains have got crossed. You think: "Open the door", and you walk into it instead!

Usually if we do something stupid, we laugh at ourselves, or go red and get cross! The great thing about 'the stupid man' is that we can laugh at *him* instead!

Did you hear about the stupid man who
came home from the car wash soaking wet?
He forgot to take the car!

Why did the stupid man stand at the mirror with
his eyes closed?
To see what he looked like with his eyes shut!

Comedy is full of characters who do stupid things that make us laugh. Think of Mr Bean, George of the Jungle, or Harry in *Third Rock from the Sun*.

Like 'the stupid man', they remind us how stupid *we* are sometimes. Luckily, they're much more stupid that we can ever be!

I think.

PERFORMANCE TIP:
Say the feed line in your normal voice. Then say the punchline in a 'stupid' voice.

MAKE YOUR OWN!

Now make your own STUPID jokes. Match each feed line to one of the punchlines. Then turn the page to see if you are a right comedian!

Why did the stupid boy go to a school for cows?
He wanted . . .

a pat on the head!
a saucer of milk!
to ring the bell!

Why did the stupid boy order alphabetti spaghetti?
He wanted . . .

a full tummy!
to eat his words!
to cook the books!

Why did the stupid lady sell her crystal ball?
She couldn't . . .

afford to keep it!
see any future in it!
get a signal!

YOU CRACKED IT!

Why did the stupid boy go to a school for cows?
He wanted a pat on the head!

Why did the stupid boy order alphabetti
spaghetti?
He wanted to eat his words!

Why did the stupid lady sell her crystal ball?
She couldn't see any future in it!

MAKE YOUR OWN!

Did your hear about the stupid man who ran into a
bar — and broke three ribs?

He was thirsty!
It was Thursday!
It was an iron bar!

Did you hear about the stupid lady who put her
house on the market?

She joined the circus!
She squashed 8 greengrocers!
She moved to Manchester!

Did you hear about the stupid boy whose brain was
in perfect condition?

It had never been used!
He thought he was a gorilla!
He was actually very clever!

YOU CRACKED IT!

Did your hear about the stupid man who ran into a
bar – and broke three ribs?
It was an iron bar!

Did you hear about the stupid lady who put her
house on the market?
She squashed 8 greengrocers!

Did you hear about the stupid boy whose brain was
in perfect condition?
It had never been used!

MAKE YOUR OWN!

What did the stupid boy call his pet tortoise?

Justin!
Patch!
Speedy!

Why did the stupid ghost spend the night outside his house?

It was Sunday!
He'd forgotten his door key!
The dog was missing!

Why did the stupid man drive his car into the sea?

To check his tyres weren't punctured!
To visit the fishes!
He was a learner!

YOU CRACKED IT!

What did the stupid boy call his pet tortoise?
Speedy!

Why did the stupid ghost spend the night outside
his house?
He'd forgotten his door key!

Why did the stupid man drive his car into the sea?
To check his tyres weren't punctured!

NOW MAKE 'EM LAUGH

Why did the stupid girl stare at her fish fingers?
She didn't know fish HAD fingers?

Did you hear about the stupid man
who tried to join MI5?
He took a wrong turn and ended up on the M25!

What did the stupid man call his pet goldfish?
Rover!

Did you hear about the stupid man
who ironed his house?
He wanted to live in a flat!

Why did the stupid man have his phone cut off?
He kept hearing voices!

Why did the stupid boy leave the classroom?
His pen ran out, and he went after it!

Why did the stupid man stop playing bowls?
He couldn't find a bowl big enough to play in!

Why did the stupid man put a fish on his shoulder?
He had a chip on the other shoulder!

Why did the stupid man take his dustbin to a
restaurant?
He wanted to leave a tip!

Why did the stupid diamond thief carry two
bricks?
Because the jeweller's window was double-glazed!

What did the stupid man do when he was
told he had a flea in his ear?
He shot it!

Why was the stupid man kept in suspense?
I'll tell you next week!

Why did the stupid man buy 10 bottles of olive oil?
To stop his olives going rusty!

Why did the stupid man wear an anorak,
a mackintosh and a cagoule to paint his house?
The tin said 'Put on three coats'!

Why did the stupid man park his car
on a double-yellow line?
The road sign said 'Fine for parking'!

Why did the stupid man take a pencil
to bed with him every night?
So he could draw the curtains!

Did you hear about the stupid plastic surgeon?
He sat on the radiator and melted!

Why did the stupid girl cut her fingers off?
She wanted to write shorthand!

Why did the stupid man give up shoplifting?
He couldn't lift up the shop!

Why wouldn't the stupid boy go to the end of the queue?
He said there was somebody there already!

Why did the stupid man put a lump of sugar under
his pillow?
So he would have sweet dreams!

Why was the stupid sailor thrown out
of the submarine service?
He always slept with the windows open!

Why did the stupid sailor push his clothes
through a porthole every night?
So he'd have clean clothes in the morning!

Why did the stupid sword-swallower
swallow an umbrella?
He was putting something away for a rainy day!

Did you hear about the stupid man
who tried to blow up a car?
He burnt his lips on the exhaust pipe!

Why did the stupid man have a jelly in one ear,
and custard in the other?
He was a trifle deaf!

Did you hear about the stupid man
who sits under his bed all night?
I think he's a little potty!

Why did the stupid man take his printer to be
fixed?
He said the 'O' kept printing upside down!

Did you hear about the stupid man who crashed
the car
and hit his head on his windscreen?
He didn't have time to blow up his airbag!

Why did the stupid boys stand in the doorway?
They wanted to play draughts!

What does the stupid man play in the orchestra?
The fool!

Why did the stupid man put a lamp on his sundial?
So he could tell the time at night!

Teachers &
Pupils

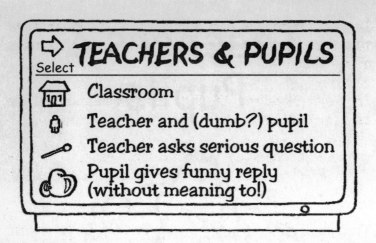

Did you know . . . in your life you'll spend about 15,000 hours at school?

In fact, teachers and pupils spend so much time together that someone was bound to make up jokes about them!

In 'T&P' jokes the teacher asks somebody in the class a question:

> Teacher: Jenny, what's the largest
> type of mouse in the world?
> Jenny: The Hippopota-mouse!

The teacher's question isn't funny (as if!). And sometimes the pupil's reply is only funny by accident . . .

> Teacher: James, name the four seasons.
> James: Salt, pepper, mustard and vinegar!

Or he doesn't understand the question . . .

> Teacher: Nat, how do you spell 'wrong'?
> Nat: R-O-N-G.
> Teacher: That's wrong.
> Nat: Exactly!

Or he's being cheeky . . .

Teacher: What's your name, boy?
Pupil: Michael.
Teacher: Say 'sir'!
Pupil: OK, Sir Michael!

Or making an excuse!

Teacher: Why are you late, Ellie?
Ellie: I threw away my alarm clock, Miss.
Teacher: But why did you throw away your clock?
Ellie: It kept going off when I was asleep!

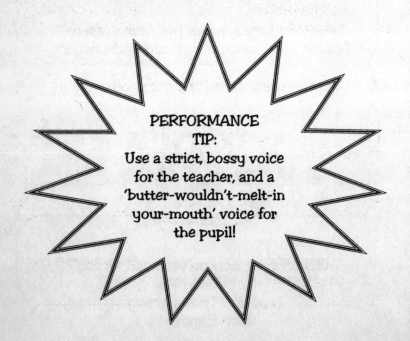

PERFORMANCE
TIP:
Use a strict, bossy voice
for the teacher, and a
'butter-wouldn't-melt-in
your-mouth' voice for
the pupil!

MAKE YOUR OWN

Draw a line between the punchline and the correct feed line to make a whole joke!

TEACHER

PUPIL

Your handwriting is terrible!

What? And risk getting bitten?

What do geese eat?

If it was better, you'd know I can't spell!

When you yawn, put your hand to your mouth!

Gooseberries?

YOU CRACKED IT!

TEACHER

PUPIL

Your handwriting is terrible!

What? And risk getting bitten?

What do geese eat?

If it was better, you'd know I can't spell!

When you yawn, put your hand to your mouth!

Gooseberries?

MAKE YOUR OWN

TEACHER

PUPIL

Why are you scratching yourself?

'Cos no one else knows where I itch!

Why do you always write the wrong answers?

I hope you didn't too!

I hope I didn't see you cheating!

'Cos you always set the wrong questions!

YOU CRACKED IT!

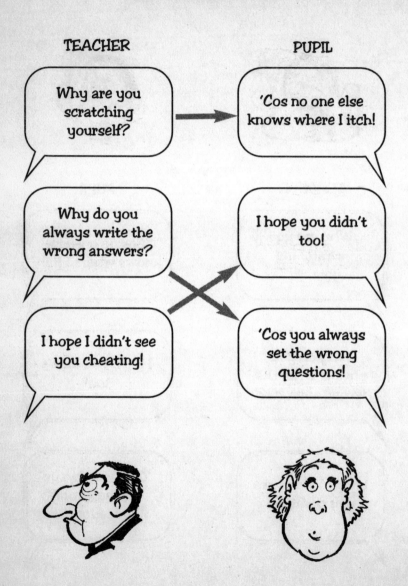

MAKE YOUR OWN

TEACHER

PUPIL

Wipe that mud off your shoes!

A bird that steals, Miss!

How do people dress in Iceland?

But I'm not wearing any shoes!

What's a robin?

Quickly!

YOU CRACKED IT!

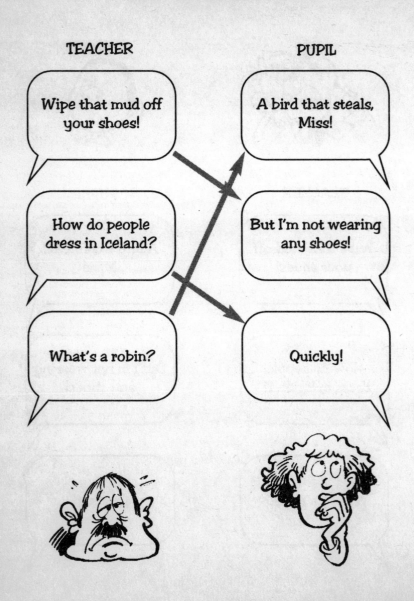

MAKE YOUR OWN

TEACHER PUPIL

What's a computer byte?

I'm not late, I'm early for tomorrow!

Have you been an idiot your whole life?

Not yet!

It's 2:30! Why are you so late?

I didn't know they had teeth!

YOU CRACKED IT!

MAKE YOUR OWN

TEACHER   PUPIL

Why were you late for school?

24 – E.T.'s gone home!

What is a bison?

Sorry, Miss, I must have over-washed!

How many letters are there in the alphabet?

It's what you wash your hands in!

YOU CRACKED IT!

TEACHER

PUPIL

Why were you late for school?

24 – E.T.'s gone home!

What is a bison?

Sorry, Miss, I must have over-washed!

How many letters are there in the alphabet?

It's what you wash your hands in!

MAKE YOUR OWN

TEACHER   PUPIL

Can you name 7 animals from India?

The day after Wednesday?

What does 'thirsty' mean?

At the bottom?

Where was the Magna Carta signed?

Six tigers and an elephant!

YOU CRACKED IT!

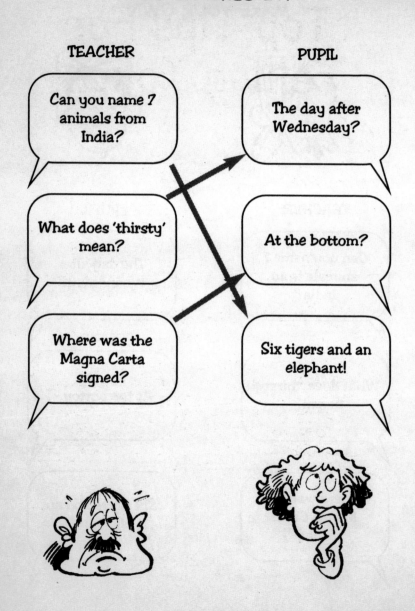

Top Tips For Telling Jokes!

LEARN IT!

The best way to tell jokes is to know them really well!

WHAT DO YOU GET IF YOU CROSS... NO NOT A GOAT, A SHEEP... WITH A WODLLY JUMPER... NO THAT'S THE PUNCHLINE...

PRACTISE IT!

Practice stops you laughing at a joke when you should be telling it.

SO THE CAMEL... HA HA... THE CAMEL SAID... IT'S SO FUNNY... THE CAMEL, YOU SEE... HA HA HA

CHOOSE YOUR AUDIENCE!

Try to choose the right joke for the right listener!

CHOOSE YOUR MOMENT!

If people aren't in the mood for a joke they just won't think it's funny.

TIMING

Timing is the real secret of telling a joke.

1. Wait till people are paying attention
2. Tell the joke slowly and clearly
3. Leave pauses so the audience have to wait for your next line, especially the punch-line
4. Don't leave people enough time to think of the answer, or shout it out.
5. Never laugh at your own jokes — just smile.

RIDE THE WAVE

Once people start laughing they WANT to carry on, so tell another joke during the laughter – this is called 'riding the wave'.

EMERGENCY KIT

If no one laughs, don't 'dry' – have a stock of funny lines about it!

Waiter, Waiter!

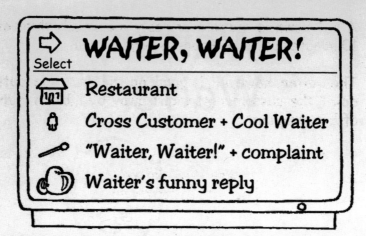

'Waiter, Waiter' jokes are set in a restaurant. A cross customer complains, and the waiter gives a clever reply:

Why is it funny? Because the waiter is good at PUT-DOWNS!

A 'put-down' is that clever reply you usually think of 10 minutes after someone is rude to you!

The waiter, however, is quick on the draw. He 'puts down' the customer straight away by making FUN of his complaint:

Waiter, Waiter!
There's a fly in my soup!

Keep quiet, sir,
or everyone will want one!

OR

Don't worry, sir,
they don't drink much.

OR

You're quite wrong, sir.
It's got eight legs, see?

OR

What do you want me to do,
Call a lifeguard?

Of course, we don't want the Waiter to have ALL the best replies! Sometimes — just sometimes — the customer has the last laugh:

Waiter, Waiter!
How long have you worked here?
About three weeks, sir.
Then it wasn't you who took my order!

After all, the customer IS probably right. It is the WORST restaurant in the world!

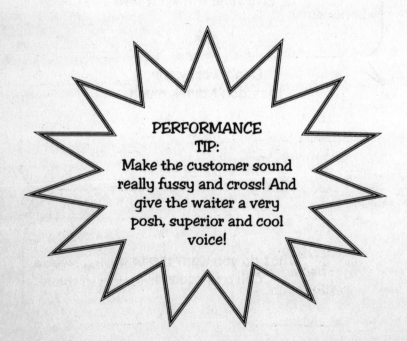

PERFORMANCE
TIP:
Make the customer sound
really fussy and cross! And
give the waiter a very
posh, superior and cool
voice!

MAKE YOUR OWN

Now make your own jokes! There are three waiters below and three customers. But which waiter is talking to which customer?

CUSTOMER

Waiter, Waiter! Is this steak rare?

Waiter, Waiter! Are there snails on the menu?

Waiter, Waiter! That bacon was really tough!

WAITER

Yes, they must have escaped from the pan!

You just ate your wristwatch sir!

No, madam, we've got lots of them!

YOU CRACKED IT!

CUSTOMER

WAITER

Waiter, Waiter! Is this steak rare?

Yes, they must have escaped from the pan!

Waiter, Waiter! Are there snails on the menu?

You just ate your wristwatch sir!

Waiter, Waiter! That bacon was really tough!

No, madam, we've got lots of them!

MAKE YOUR OWN

Which waiter is talking to which customer in these three jokes?

CUSTOMER

WAITER

Waiter, Waiter! There's a button in my potato!

I didn't ask for a nosebleed, did I, madam?

Waiter, Waiter! A fly is laying eggs in my soup!

Yes, sir. It's a 'jacket' potato!

Waiter, Waiter! I didn't ask for ketchup!

Isn't nature just wonderful, madam?

YOU CRACKED IT!

CUSTOMER   **WAITER**

Waiter, Waiter!
There's a button in
my potato!

I didn't ask for a
nosebleed, did I,
madam?

Waiter, Waiter!
A fly is laying eggs
in my soup!

Yes, sir. It's a 'jacket'
potato!

Waiter, Waiter!
I didn't ask for
ketchup!

Isn't nature just
wonderful,
madam?

MAKE YOUR OWN

Which waiter is talking to which customer in these three jokes?

CUSTOMER   WAITER

Waiter, Waiter! I'd like pie and then some milk.

Well, madam, we used to call it 'Rover'!

Waiter, Waiter! Do you call this meat beef?

I'm a waiter, not a blooming vet!

Waiter, Waiter! This chicken is diseased!

Have the milk first, sir, it's about to go off!

YOU CRACKED IT!

CUSTOMER   **WAITER**

> Waiter, Waiter! I'd like pie and then some milk.

> Well, madam, we used to call it 'Rover'!

> Waiter, Waiter! Do you call this meat beef?

> I'm a waiter, not a blooming vet!

> Waiter, Waiter! This chicken is diseased!

> Have the milk first, sir, it's about to go off!

NOW MAKE 'EM LAUGH

Waiter, Waiter!
There's a rat in this pie!
Sorry, sir, no pets allowed!

Waiter, Waiter!
There's a beetle on my chop!
They just don't care what they eat, do they sir?

Waiter, Waiter!
There are teeth marks in my snails!
It's the chef, madam. He's always biting his snails!

Waiter, Waiter!
There's a fly in my custard!
I'll fetch him a spoon, sir.

Waiter, Waiter!
What would you recommend tonight?
There's a Chinese two doors down.

Waiter, Waiter!
There's a fly in my fruit salad!
Yes, madam, it's the rotten apples that attract
them!

Waiter, Waiter!
I can't eat this stuff, send for the manager!
It's no use, sir, he won't eat it either.

Waiter, Waiter!
There's a film on my glass!
Then why don't you shut up and watch it?

Waiter, Waiter!
There's a cake in my soup!
That's muffin to worry about, sir!

Waiter, Waiter!
This cheese is full of holes!
Don't complain, madam,
it used to be full of maggots!

Waiter, Waiter! Is this salmon fresh?
I caught it myself, sir.
Yes, but when did you catch it?
When it fell off the counter just now!

Waiter, Waiter!
The service in here is terrible.
This is a church, sir,
the restaurant's next door.

Waiter, Waiter!
There's a hair in my honey!
It must have dropped off the comb, sir.

Waiter, Waiter!
That dog just ran off with my sausages!
Yes, they're very popular, sir.

Waiter, Waiter!
There's a twig in my soup!
Yes, madam,
we've got branches everywhere!

Waiter, Waiter!
I asked for bread with my sausages.
The bread's in the sausages, madam.

Waiter, Waiter!
There's no chicken in this chicken pie!
Do you expect dog in dog biscuits, madam?

Waiter, Waiter!
There's soap in this custard!
That's to help wash it down, sir!

Waiter, Waiter!
Are you any good at maths?
Well, I know my tables, madam!

Waiter, Waiter!
Is my dinner hot?
It should be, sir. It's been on fire since seven
o'clock!

Waiter, Waiter!
I want to see the chef immediately!
I'm afraid he's gone out for dinner, madam!

Waiter, Waiter!
There's only one sausage on my plate!
Hang on, sir, I'll cut it in two for you!

Waiter, Waiter!
How long will my sausages be?
About eight centimetres, sir!

Waiter, Waiter!
I'd like a beer and a piece of fish.
Fillet?
Yes — right to the top of the glass!

Waiter, Waiter!
The crust on that pie was very tough!
That wasn't the crust, sir, it was the plate!

Waiter, Waiter!
This steak is rare. I said 'well done'!
I know sir, and the chef says 'thank you'!

Waiter, Waiter!
This plate is wet!
That's your soup, sir.

Waiter, Waiter!
This beer is all cloudy!
It certainly is not, sir!
It's the glass that's all cloudy.

And some customer winners!

Waiter, Waiter!
Bring me some cold soup, stale bread,
and a dirty knife and fork.
We don't serve meals like that, madam.
Well you did yesterday!

Waiter, Waiter!
Would you bring my bill, please.
And how did you find your lunch, sir?
With a magnifying glass.

Waiter, Waiter!
What on earth do you call this?
That's bean soup, madam.
I don't care what it's been — what is it now?

Waiter, Waiter!
I can't drink this soup!
How come?
You haven't brought me a spoon, you idiot!

What Do You Call . . . ?

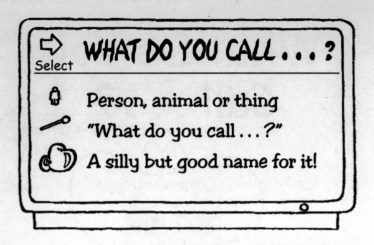

What do you call . . .
the Invisible Man's mummy and daddy?

TransParents!

What's the first thing you ever said? It was probably 'Mama' or 'Dada'. You looked at those strange hairy things looming over you and gave them a NAME.

Then you looked around and NAMED the things you saw:

Now you're older you give your pet a NEW NAME, your best friend a NICKNAME and your teacher a RUDE NAME!

'What do you call . . . ?' jokes are all about giving SILLY NAMES to things that don't have a name!

What do you call . . .
a donkey with three legs?

A wonkey!

A 'wonkey' is a SILLY name. But it's also a really GOOD name, because three-legged chairs or tables are wonky, which sounds like 'donkey'. It just sounds right!

What do you call a reindeer with one eye?
No idea!
(No-eye deer)

What do you call a dead reindeer with one eye?
Still no idea!

Every day people have to make up NEW names for new things:

Inventions
Laszlo Biro invented the ballpoint pen – and named it the BIRO!

Weather
Hurricanes are given names in alphabetical order, taking turns to be a boy's name or a girl's name – like Hurricane Charlie!

Movies
Films like *STAR WARS* are named to tell you what the film's about and to make you want to see it!

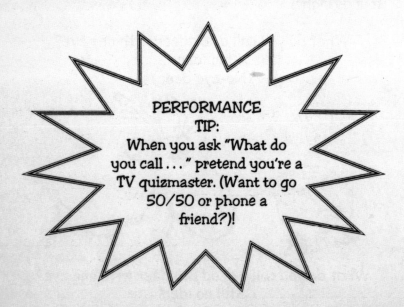

PERFORMANCE
TIP:
When you ask "What do you call . . . " pretend you're a TV quizmaster. (Want to go 50/50 or phone a friend?)!

MAKE YOUR OWN

Now make your own 'What do you call . . . ?' jokes.
Fill in the blanks using *some* of the words at the
bottom of the page.

What do you call . . .
a multi-storey pig pen?

(   )

What do you call . . .
a fan who shouts loudly at matches?

(   )

What do you call . . .
an artist who painted sitting on the fridge?

(   )

Bottychilly, a hamburglar, a styscraper,
a footbawler, Tiny

YOU CRACKED IT!

What do you call . . .
a multi-storey pig pen?

> A styscraper!

What do you call . . .
a fan who shouts loudly at matches?

> A footbawler!

What do you call . . .
an artist who painted sitting on the fridge?

> Bottychilly!

MAKE YOUR OWN

What do you call . . .
a short elephant?

What do you call . . .
a cat wearing shoes?

What do you call . . .
a cow in the Antarctic?

*an eskimoo, Puss-in-Boots, a snowman, truncated,
purrfect*

YOU CRACKED IT!

What do you call . . .
a short elephant?

Truncated!

What do you call . . .
a cat wearing shoes?

Puss-in-Boots!

What do you call . . .
a cow in the Antarctic?

An eskimoo!

MAKE YOUR OWN

What do you call . . .
a dinosaur that likes heavy metal music?

What do you call . . .
a pop group on Mars?

What do you call . . .
a pig with no clothes on?

streaky bacon, T. Rocks, Pluto, a hambug, the
Space Girls

YOU CRACKED IT!

What do you call . . .
a dinosaur that likes heavy metal music?

T. Rocks!

What do you call . . .
a pop group on Mars?

The Space Girls!

What do you call . . .
a pig with no clothes on?

Streaky bacon!

MAKE YOUR OWN

What do you call . . .
two witches who are friends?

What do you call . . .
a whale that's crying?

What do you call . . .
a clam that won't share?

very shellfish, Lily, broom-mates, a blubber, Sir

YOU CRACKED IT!

What do you call . . .
two witches who are friends?

Broom-mates!

What do you call . . .
a whale that's crying?

A blubber!

What do you call . . .
a clam that won't share?

Very shellfish!

NOW MAKE 'EM LAUGH

What do you call . . .
a lion with no eyes?
A Lon!

What do you call . . .
a snowman with a suntan?
A puddle!

What do you call . . .
a camel without a hump?
Humphrey!

What do you call . . .
a fish that eats people two by two?
Noah's shark!

What do you call . . .
a baby who can write?
A dribbler scribbler!

What do you call . . .
a racehorse with six legs?
A winner!

What do you call . . .
a teacher with paws of a grizzly and
the teeth of a Rottweiler?
Sir!

What do you call . . .
people who watch Sumo Wrestling?
Weight Watchers!

What do you call . . .
an elephant in a phone box?
Stuck!

What do you call . . .
an Alsatian wearing a jumper?
A plain clothes police dog!

What do you call . . .
a big white animal with a hole in its middle?
A polo bear!

What do you call . . .
sheep that write to each other?
Pen friends!

What do you call . . .
a woman with one leg?
Eileen!

What do you call . . .
a hag who stops cars with her thumb?
A witch-hiker!

What do you call . . .
a wizard from outer space?
A flying sorcerer!

What do you call . . .
a ghost that saves penalties?
A ghou-keeper!

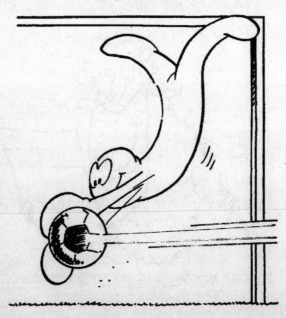

What do you call . . .
a nervous witch?
A Twitch!

What do you call . . .
a demon that slurps its food?
A gobblin'.

What do you call . . .
a skeleton that won't get up in the morning?
Lazy bones!

What do you call . . .
a ghost who lives in Buckingham Palace?
The Spook of Edinburgh!

What do you call . . .
a grasshopper with no legs?
A grasshovver!

What do you call . . .
a dog owned by Dracula?
A bloodhound!

What do you call . . .
a wizard who's been buried in the ground for
centuries?
Pete!

What do you call . . .
a tropical fruity computer?
A pine-Apple Mac!

What do you call . . .
an ant that hates going to school?
A tru-ant!

What do you call . . .
a hairy beast with clothes on?
A wearwolf!

What do you call . . .
a hairy beast that's lost?
A where?wolf!

What do you call . . .
the middle of a graveyard?
Dead centre!

What do you call . . .
a vampire after it's one year old?
A two-year-old vampire!

What do you call . . .
a skeleton in a snowstorm?
A numbskull!

What do you call . . .
a gun that fires jelly and custard?
A t-rifle!

What do you call . . .
a dinosaur who babysits?
A Nannysaurus!